D1573272

AVERROES
(IBN RUSHD)

Muslim Scholar, Philosopher, and
Physician of the Twelfth Century

Great Muslim Philosophers and Scientists of the Middle Ages™

AVERROES
(IBN RUSHD)

Muslim Scholar, Philosopher, and
Physician of the Twelfth Century

Liz Sonneborn

The Rosen Publishing Group, Inc., New York

Published in 2006 by The Rosen Publishing Group, Inc.
29 East 21st Street, New York, NY 10010

First Edition

Library of Congress Cataloging-in-Publication Data

Sonneborn, Liz.
Averroes (Ibn Rushd): Muslim scholar, philosopher, and physician of the twelfth century/Liz Sonneborn.—1st ed.
    p. cm.—(Great Muslim philosophers and scientists of the Middle Ages)
Includes bibliographical references and index.
ISBN 1-4042-0514-4 (library binding)
1. Averroës, 1126-1198. 2. Philosophy, Medieval. 3. Philosophy, Islamic.
I. Title. II. Series.

B749.Z7S65 2006
181'.92—dc22

                               2005011816

Manufactured in the United States of America

Unless otherwise attributed, all quoted material comes from *Averroes: His Life, Works and Influence* by Majid Fakhry.

On the cover: Averroes is pictured here in a detail from the fresco entitled *Triumph of St. Thomas Aquinas* in the Spanish Chapel, Santa Maria Novella, in Florence, Italy.

CONTENTS

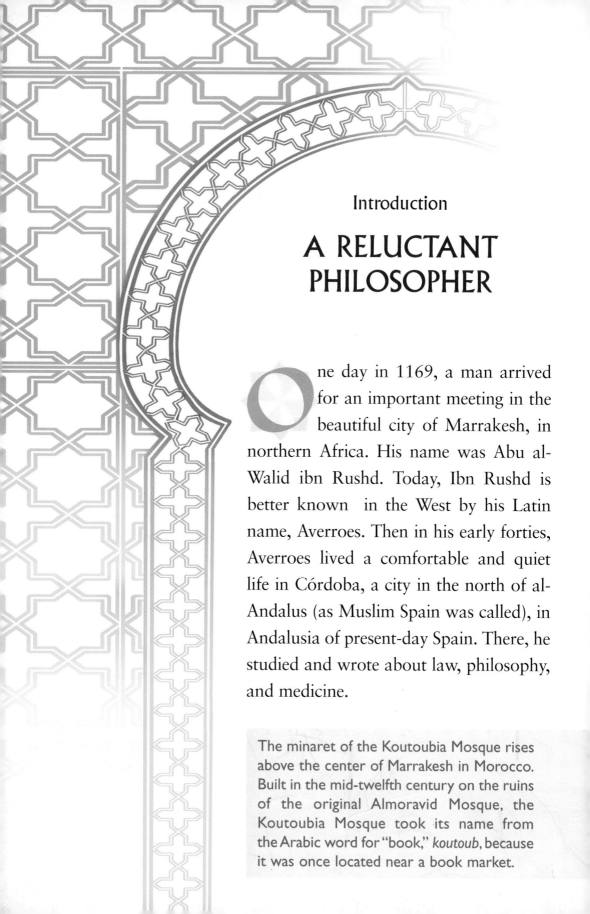

Introduction

A RELUCTANT PHILOSOPHER

One day in 1169, a man arrived for an important meeting in the beautiful city of Marrakesh, in northern Africa. His name was Abu al-Walid ibn Rushd. Today, Ibn Rushd is better known in the West by his Latin name, Averroes. Then in his early forties, Averroes lived a comfortable and quiet life in Córdoba, a city in the north of al-Andalus (as Muslim Spain was called), in Andalusia of present-day Spain. There, he studied and wrote about law, philosophy, and medicine.

The minaret of the Koutoubia Mosque rises above the center of Marrakesh in Morocco. Built in the mid-twelfth century on the ruins of the original Almoravid Mosque, the Koutoubia Mosque took its name from the Arabic word for "book," *koutoub*, because it was once located near a book market.

Averroes had been invited to meet with Abu Yaqub Yusuf, who in the year before had become the second caliph, or ruler, of the Almohad dynasty. At that time, the Almohads controlled a large empire that included what is now northern Africa and southern Spain.

When Averroes arrived, he saw that the caliph already had another guest, Averroes' old friend and teacher Abu Bakr ibn Tufayl. Like Averroes, Ibn Tufayl was a scholar. In addition to being a physician, he studied the works of Muslim philosophers. Ibn Tufayl was particularly interested in the writing of Abu Ali al-Husain ibn Sina, also known as Avicenna (980–1037). Avicenna was an expert in the works of Aristotle, a philosopher who lived in ancient Greece some 1,400 years earlier.

QUESTIONS ABOUT CREATION

As the meeting began, Averroes had no idea what to expect from the caliph. But soon, he became very nervous. According to Majid Fakhry's *Averroes: His Life, Works and Influence* (2001), the caliph immediately began asking Averroes some extremely disturbing questions: "What do the philosophers believe regarding heaven? Is it eternal or created in time?"

Such questions were hardly new. Long ago, the ancient Greek philosophers had developed their own answers. Plato

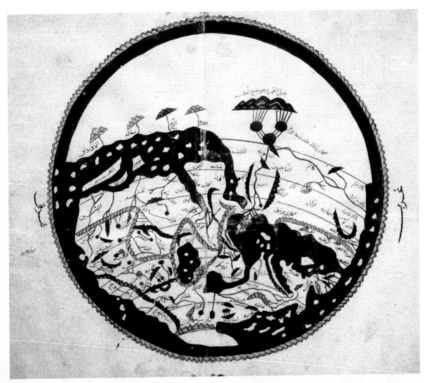

Muslim geographer Abu Abd Allah Muhammad al-Idrisi (1100–1164) made this map of the world for a book he completed for King Roger II of Sicily in 1154. Later known as *Roger's Book (Kitab Rujar)*, it was written in Arabic and Latin. Al-Idrisi based his maps on the cartographic studies of the Greek astronomer Claudius Ptolemy of the second century. Al-Idrisi drew this map with south being at the top, the Arabian Peninsula near the top, Mecca (Makkah) at the center, and Europe at the bottom.

had argued that the world had a definite beginning, while Aristotle maintained it had always existed. Many Muslim religious scholars, however, vehemently denounced both philosophers' arguments in this regard. In these scholars' eyes, the ideas advanced by the Greeks directly contradicted the Qur'an (also known as the Koran), the holy scripture of Islam, in many ways—from their views on the origin of the world to their ideas about an afterlife. Muslims believed that the Qur'an was the word of God, delivered to humankind by the prophet Muhammad. To contradict the Qur'an was, therefore, an offense against God.

Understandably, Averroes was leery of the caliph's questions. Was the caliph trying to trap him into saying something inappropriate? What would the caliph do if Averroes said something with which he did not agree?

Averroes decided to play it safe. As recounted by Oliver Leaman in *Averroes and His Philosophy* (1998), Averroes developed a strategy: "I began to make excuses and deny that I had ever concerned myself with philosophic learning; for I did not know what Ibn Tufayl had told him on the subject."

The caliph saw Averroes' discomfort and tried to set his mind at ease. He explained at length his own understanding of the views of Greek philosophers as well as the charges against them leveled by great Muslim thinkers. As a young man, Abu Yaqub had spent some time in the city of Seville in al-Andalus. There, he socialized with the philosophers, scholars, and poets, absorbing their knowledge and developing an appetite for more. Through his own studies, the caliph had become something of an expert on both Greek and Muslim philosophers. Averroes was quite impressed. He later told a friend that he found in the caliph "a profuseness of learning [he] did not suspect in a specialist in that field."

IMPRESSING THE CALIPH

Convinced the caliph wanted an open discussion, Averroes began to expound his own studies in philosophy. The caliph was excited by his expertise. According to Leaman in *Averroes and His Philosophy*, Averroes later recalled that the get-together ended on a happy note: "Thus he continued to set me at ease until I spoke, and he learned what was my competence in that subject; and when I withdrew he ordered for me a gift of money, a magnificent robe of honor and a steed!"

The caliph had good reason to be pleased. Before the meeting, Abu Yaqub had been struggling in his quest to master Greek philosophy. He was particularly puzzled by many of Aristotle's texts, which he read in Arabic translations from the original Greek. The caliph had asked Ibn Tufayl to write commentaries on Aristotle to help him interpret the Greek philosopher's meaning. Ibn Tufayl had declined, saying he was too old and too busy to take on such a difficult project. He instead recommended Averroes for the job.

Uod quidez igit neqz
factum est omne celum
neqz contingit corrupi
queadmoduz quidam
dicunt ipsuz: sed e vnū
7 sempiternū principi
um 7 psumationez ha
bens totius eterni non
habens autē 7 ptinens
in seipo infinitū tēpus
ex dictis licet accipere side 7 per opinionē eaz q
ab aliter dicentibus 7 generantibus ipsum. si. n.
sic quidē habē contingit sm quē autez illi factū
esse dicunt non cōtingit magnam vtiqz habebit
7 hoc inclinationem ad sidem de imortalitate
ipsius 7 sempiternitate.

¶ Jam declarauimus sermonibus sufficientib°
7 sortibus demonstrationibus q celum non sit
ex elemēto: 7 q impossibile est ut cadat sub cor
ruptione sed semper erit eternum 7 fuit sine prin
cipio 7 sine fine per omnia secula 7 e causa tpis
infiniti 7 est cōtinens ipsū. desiderans autē bene
poterit scire q celum est sicut diximus ex verbis
dicentiū celū esse sub generatione. si eni possibi
le est ut celuz sicut diximus 7 impossibile est sm
q alij dicūt hoc etiā confirmat sermonē nostruz
q celum sit eternū non corruptibile.

Com.j. ¶ Idest hoc quod dixit qi non sit ex elemento duo
bus modis itelligit: aut quia nō cōponit ex materia 7 sor
ma sicut alia corpora simplicia: aut quia nō componitur

This page of Averroes' commentary on Aristotle's work *Opera Latina* comes from a 1483 to 1484 Latin translation. Caliph Abu Yaqub Yusuf originally had asked Averroes' teacher Abu Bakr ibn Tufayl to summarize the great Greek philosopher's works, but Ibn Tufayl recommended Averroes for the project. Averroes agreed to take on the huge responsibility, and his commentaries became pivotal to world history because Averroes helped introduce Aristotelian thought to Europe.

Ibn Tufayl then set about convincing Averroes of the project's worth. As recorded by Leaman, Ibn Tufayl explained,

> If someone would tackle these books, summarize them and expound their aims, after understanding them thoroughly, it would be easier for people to grasp them . . . I expect you will be equal to it, from what I know of the excellence of your mind, the purity of your nature, and the intensity of your application to science.

To the caliph's delight, Averroes agreed to devote himself to the study of Aristotle. The decision changed the course of Averroes' life. For years to come, he wrote comprehensive commentaries on the great Greek philosopher, ranging from short paraphrases of Aristotle's words to lengthy, line-by-line analyses approachable by only the most learned scholars.

Averroes' decision also changed the course of world culture. In time, his commentaries would introduce Europe to the breadth of Greek philosophy. As one of the greatest interpreters of Aristotle's philosophy, Averroes and his work would forge a crucial link between ancient and modern thought.

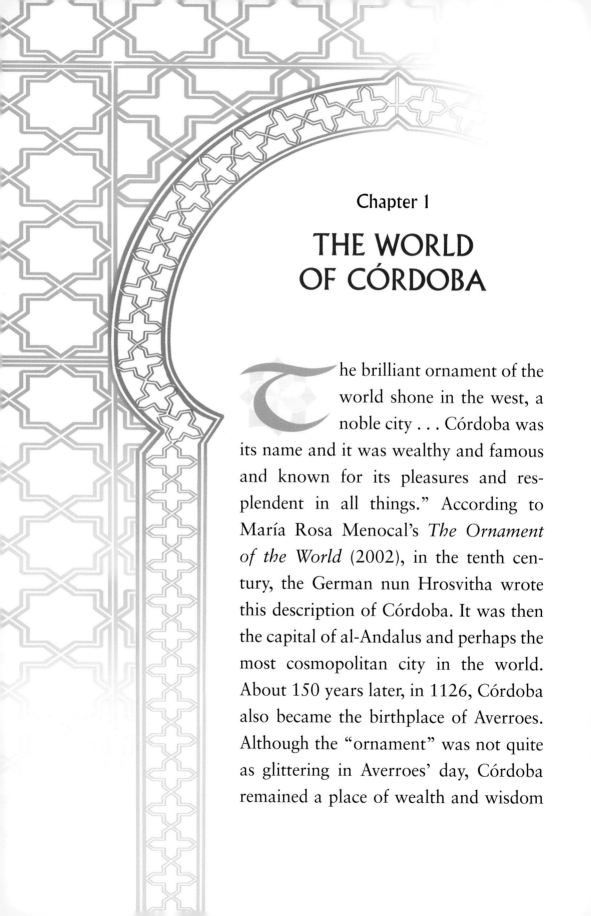

Chapter 1

THE WORLD OF CÓRDOBA

he brilliant ornament of the world shone in the west, a noble city . . . Córdoba was its name and it was wealthy and famous and known for its pleasures and resplendent in all things." According to María Rosa Menocal's *The Ornament of the World* (2002), in the tenth century, the German nun Hrosvitha wrote this description of Córdoba. It was then the capital of al-Andalus and perhaps the most cosmopolitan city in the world. About 150 years later, in 1126, Córdoba also became the birthplace of Averroes. Although the "ornament" was not quite as glittering in Averroes' day, Córdoba remained a place of wealth and wisdom that fostered Averroes' emergence as one of the greatest thinkers of his time.

THE PROPHET

The story of Averroes' Córdoba has its roots in a faraway place and time—the Arabian Peninsula during the sixth century. At that time, Arabia was not unified, either politically or religiously. Its population included Christians and Jews, as well as people who belonged to local cults that worshipped natural forces and objects as deities. There were some urban centers in Arabia, but many areas were covered by deserts

Three musicians and court life in al-Andalus are depicted on this ivory pyxis, a covered container for perfumes and salves, which is from Madinat al-Zahra and dates from around 968. Some of the finest ivories made in the tenth century were produced in the palace workshop at Madinat al-Zahra, a city located west of Córdoba.

and, therefore, could not support large populations. The people of the deserts were largely nomads. Many were members of tribes led by hereditary leaders.

In the town of Mecca (Makkah) in western Arabia, Muhammad ibn Abd Allah was born in about 570. He

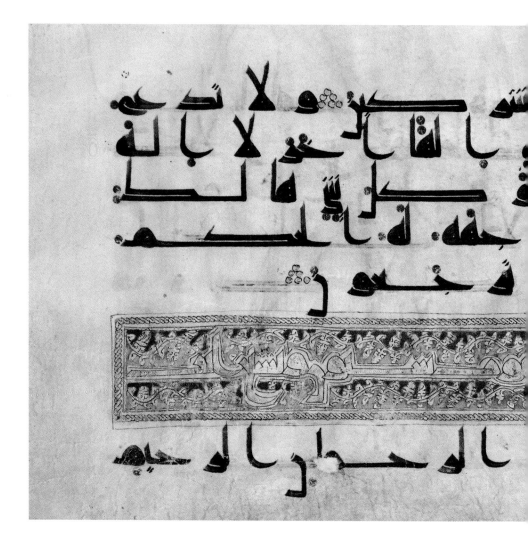

belonged to the Quraysh tribe, which then controlled Mecca. The Quraysh oversaw a shrine there called the Kabah, which had become associated with many tribal gods.

Muslims believe that around 610, Muhammad was visited by the angel Gabriel, who told him he was chosen to be God's prophet. At first frightened, he came to accept this new role.

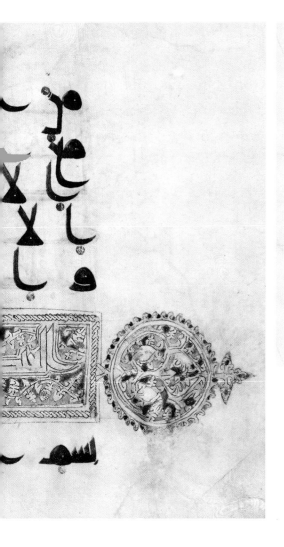

This page from the Qur'an shows the heading of Sura 29, al-Ankaboot, or "The Spider," and was written perhaps in Iraq around 911. The Sura, one of 114 chapters or sections that makes up the Qur'an, contains sixty-nine *ayat*, or verses. It was named al-Ankaboot because of verse forty-one, which mentions the frailty of false gods and compares them to the fragility of a spiderweb. The Qur'an is the sacred book of Islam, which Muslims believe to be the word of God revealed to Muhammad through the angel Gabriel.

The revelations that he then received were compiled into a book called the Qur'an. The Qur'an is the sacred scripture of Islam, which, along with Judaism and Christianity, is one of the three great monotheistic religions in the world today. Islam's followers, known as Muslims, hold that the Qur'an is the literal word of God.

The Qur'an calls on Muslims to worship the One God and requires them to behave according to certain rules during their life on earth. Muslims believe that they can achieve salvation and be sent to heaven after death only by adhering to certain beliefs regarding God, angels, prophets, holy books, and the afterlife. They must also obey the rules for a specific set of rituals, including profession of faith, prayer, charity giving, fasting, and pilgrimages.

Muhammad began preaching his message in about 613. Devoted to the worship of the One God, his words posed a direct challenge to the beliefs of the Quraysh and other tribes. Even so, he found some followers in Mecca and other nearby towns, including Yathrib. The people of Yathrib invited Muhammad to move there and essentially become its leader. He made the journey from Mecca to Yathrib in 622. This event was called the *Hijra* (meaning "emigration"). Yathrib itself was renamed Medina (Madinah), or "city of the Prophet."

These Muslims made a pilgrimage to Mecca *(hajj)* and are visiting the cave near Mount Hira (Jabal al-Nour or "Mountain of Light"), north of Mecca, where the prophet Muhammad frequently meditated and where, according to Islam, he received his first revelations from the angel Gabriel.

THE SPREAD OF ISLAM

After the Hijra, Muhammad became a political as well as a religious leader. Under the Prophet's leadership, Medina struggled with Mecca to win the support of other towns and tribal groups. Muhammad's religious message attracted many groups to his side. When he died in 632, he held western Arabia under his sway.

Following the Prophet's death, leadership of his followers fell to a line of caliphs ("caliph" literally means "successor to the Prophet"). The first was Abu Bakr al-Asamm, Muhammad's companion and father-in-law. Through military campaigns, he brought all of Arabia into an emerging Muslim Empire. Under Abu Bakr and his successor, Umar ibn al-Khattab, Muslim rule continued to spread—to the west into the Byzantine Empire and to the east into the Sassanid (Persian)

The Umayyad caliph Abd al-Malik reformed coinage in 696. Any pictorial images that were once used in minting of coins, including portraits of rulers, were replaced with writing, such as that seen on this gold dinar. The Muslim profession of faith, the *shahada* ("There is no God but Allah, Muhammad is the messenger of Allah"), is written in Arabic in many of the coins' inscriptions.

Empire. Many of the people in these regions were neither Arab nor Muslim. Therefore, although the Muslim Empire was guided by the laws of the Qur'an, its population included people of many different ethnicities and religions.

The Muslims faced a crisis in 656, when the third caliph, Uthman ibn Affan, was murdered. He was succeeded by Ali ibn Abi Talib, Muhammad's cousin and son-in-law. But some people, including members of the Umayyad clan, who were related to Uthman, opposed Ali's rule. The two sides went to battle in 657, before Ali was assassinated in 661. Eager for the infighting to end, a majority of Muslims decided to follow Muawiyah ibn Abi Sufyan, leader of the Umayyads. A minority, though, still supported Ali and his family. They became the subgroup of Muslims known as the Shia or Shiites.

THE UMAYYAD CALIPHATE

The rule of the Umayyad family lasted fewer than 100 years. During the first years of the caliphate, the Umayyads were preoccupied with fighting their political and religious rivals within the Muslim Empire. But by the early 700s, they again began to send armies to extend Muslim rule to other lands. In the west, Muslims pushed into northern Africa. There, they found converts among the local Berber tribes in Morocco. With the help of the Berbers, Arabs led by Tariq ibn Ziyad crossed the Strait of Gibraltar and conquered much of what is now southern and western Spain from the Visigoths. Once under Muslim control, this area was given the Arabic name al-Andalus.

Despite the Umayyads' success in expanding the empire, many Muslims still challenged their rule. The Shiites and other groups continued to question the legitimacy of Umayyad rule. The Umayyads repeatedly had to put down uprisings, which only emboldened their enemies.

In 750, one group, the Abbasids, finally succeeded in overthrowing the Umayyads. (The Abbasids claimed descent from Muhammad's uncle al-Abbas ibn Abd al-Muttalib.) After defeating the Umayyads' armies in several battles, the Abbasids killed the last Umayyad caliph and his family. However, one Umayyad prince, Abd al-Rahman, managed to escape. He fled to the west, eventually finding refuge in Córdoba, the capital of al-Andalus.

THE FLOWERING OF BAGHDAD

The Abbasids were eager to establish the legitimacy of their caliphate. As a symbolic gesture, the second Abbasid caliph, Abu Jafar al-Mansur, moved the royal court from Damascus in what is now Syria to a brand-new city called Baghdad, which he built in 762 in present-day Iraq. He wanted the shift to represent a break with the corrupt Umayyad past and a movement toward a glorious new future under the Abbasid caliphs.

This page is from a late tenth-century Arabic translation of Dioscorides' *De Materia Medica* (Materials of Medicine), a book that contained the medicinal uses of more than 600 plants. Dioscorides (circa AD 40–90) was a Greek surgeon and pharmacologist. His compilation was used as the primary source for botanical terms and pharmacology for more than sixteen centuries. The page pictured here is about cinnamon.

Baghdad quickly grew into a beautiful and vibrant city. At its height in the ninth century, it was home to as many as 1 million people, an astounding population for any urban area at that time. But the Abbasids were determined to make Baghdad into something more than just a huge city. They wanted it to be the greatest cultural center, not just in the Muslim Empire but in the world.

There was a good reason to believe Baghdad could become the capital of world culture. Because of their conquests, Muslims had gained access to the scholarly and artistic traditions of an array of ancient civilizations. They possessed the literature and political scholarship of Persia, the medical and mathematical knowledge of India, the legal reasoning of the Romans, and the scientific and philosophical inquiries of the Greeks.

THE TRANSLATION MOVEMENT

Under the rule of al-Mansur, scholars began to translate Indian and Greek works. However it was his successor, Abu al-Abbas Abd Allah al-Mamun, who initiated a stunningly ambitious translation movement. He brought the greatest regional scholars to Baghdad to examine and translate the learning of the ancient world into Arabic. The Abbasids would commit a huge amount of money and time—about 200 years—to this project.

As part of the translation movement, a research center called the House of Wisdom (Bayt al-Hikma) was established in Baghdad in 830. Under the direction of Hunayn ibn Ishaq al-Ibadi, scholars collected every manuscript they could find of each work and studied them to establish a definitive text before even beginning their translation. Many of the translators were Christians from the area of what is now known as Syria. They translated the Greek text into Syriac, then other translators would translate the Syriac text into Arabic.

Although Arabic had a very simple vocabulary, it proved a remarkably good language for the communication of new ideas and abstract thoughts. As a result, it became the common language among intellectuals throughout the Muslim Empire, even among non-Arabs and non-Muslims.

The translation movement preserved many works that might have otherwise been lost. For instance, the works of the Greek philosophers Plato and Aristotle had largely been forgotten by the time the project began. Only a few fragments of their works existed in all of present-day Europe.

But Muslim scholars did more than mechanically record the literature of ancient cultures for future generations. They actively evaluated these works, interpreting them to find knowledge that they could use and, even more difficult, that they could incorporate into their culture in ways that did not conflict with the Muslim

The Great Mosque of Córdoba

In his final years, Abd al-Rahman began work on a great project to bring further and lasting glory to Córdoba. He ordered the construction of a large mosque, a Muslim house of worship. The emir's great mosque was to be a symbol of Córdoba's claim to being the new Muslim cultural center.

The architecture of the Great Mosque echoed that of another structure—the mosque the Umayyad dynasty built in Damascus when it had ruled the Muslim Empire. But Córdoba's mosque also incorporated local materials, including pillars salvaged from Roman ruins. By bringing together the old and new, the building celebrated both the Umayyads' distinguished past in the East and the dynasty's renewed power under Abd al-Rahman in the West.

The project of building the Great Mosque, or La Mezquita (the Mosque) as it is known, continued long after Abd al-Rahman's death. For the next 200 years, Umayyad emirs and caliphs added onto the mosque as Córdoba expanded and its population grew. The Great Mosque became a vast structure, with horseshoe-shaped arches decorated with alternating bands of red brick and white stone and columns made of jasper, marble, granite, and onyx. The Great Mosque's walls were adorned with intricate mosaics.

In 1236, a Christian army led by Ferdinand III of Castile invaded Córdoba. Seeing that the Great Mosque remained the most visible monument to Muslim rule, the Christians could have destroyed it. But instead Ferdinand entered the mosque and reconsecrated it as a Christian church. In the sixteenth century, the mosque was converted into a cathedral. Today, it remains a destination for thousands of tourists interested in Spain's Muslim past.

worldview. For Muslim intellectuals, theologians, and philosophers, these questions prompted debates that would continue for centuries.

THE UMAYYADS IN CÓRDOBA

During the Abbasid era, other cities in the Muslim Empire became cultural centers. But perhaps Baghdad's greatest cultural rival was Córdoba, where the Umayyad prince Abd al-Rahman had fled after the massacre of his family. There, Abd al-Rahman built an army. Calling himself the emir (commander) of Muslim Spain, he took control of al-Andalus. In 756, he established an Umayyad government in the region that lasted nearly 300 years. In 929, Abd al-Rahman III, the seventh Umayyad ruler of al-Andalus, promoted himself from emir to caliph, a direct challenge to the authority of the Abbasid rulers in Baghdad. Thereafter, the Umayyads maintained that they were the true rulers of the Muslim Empire and that its true capital was Córdoba.

For centuries, the Umayyads of Córdoba and the Abbasids of Baghdad were political rivals. Even so, scholars freely traveled between the two cities, introducing Córdoba to the books and ideas circulating in Baghdad. Al-Hakam II, also known as al-Mustansir Billah, the successor of Abd al-Rahman III, actively encouraged the importation of translations from the east. Under his reign (961–976),

Córdoba emerged as a great center for learning. The city's library had more than 400,000 books, an amazingly large collection. A well-educated man himself, al-Hakam filled his court with scholars, philosophers, and artists.

Al-Hakam's patronage certainly helped make Córdoba an incubator for new ideas. In keeping with the law, the city's long tradition of tolerance also contributed to its free-flowing intellectual atmosphere. Under the Umayyads, the people of Córdoba were subject to Muslim rule and Islamic law. But the Umayyads generally did not persecute people of other faiths. They were especially tolerant of Jews and Christians, who, like Muslims, worshipped a single God. Jews and Christians were subject to special taxes and had to worship in private. But otherwise, they were largely left to live as they chose, and many even embraced aspects of Muslim culture, particularly the Arabic language. They were a vital part of Cordoban society, adding their own perspectives to the vibrant multilingual and multicultural mix of the city at its height.

A page from an illuminated manuscript from the fourteenth century depicts al-Mansur's 997 military raid on Santiago de Compostela, the city that supposedly held the bones of Saint James. Al-Mansur spent the latter part of his rule battling Christians. He brought armies of mercenaries from North Africa to al-Andalus to help him fight his military campaigns in the Christian lands north of Córdoba.

THE END OF THE UMAYYADS

After al-Hakam's brief fifteen-year reign, his eleven-year-old son, Hisham II, became the new caliph in 976. However, real power over al-Andalus fell into the hands of the caliph's counselor, Abu Amir al-Mansur. Leading as a military ruler, al-Mansur ordered the burning of some of the books in the Córdoba library because he maintained that the ideas they contained were dangerous. But most of al-Mansur's energy was devoted to battling small Christian kingdoms to the north. To aid his military campaigns, al-Mansur hired Berber soldiers from North Africa. The Cordobans greatly resented the fact that these foreign troops had been unleashed in their lands.

When al-Mansur died in 1002, power over al-Andalus was passed on to his two sons. During the second son's reign, the Andalusians had had enough. They rebelled in 1009, and the heirs to the Umayyad dynasty were restored to the caliphate. But it was too late to return to the old order. The Umayyads gradually lost their hold on the region. The caliphate officially came to an end in 1031, as al-Andalus disintegrated into a collection of some sixty city-states, called *taifas*. The rulers of these small kingdoms fought one another constantly, all jockeying for more power.

One such king, Mutamid of Seville, asked for military aid from the Almoravids, leaders of an Islamic religious movement against growing Christian strength. These conservative Muslim Berbers were building an empire in North Africa, with its capital in Marrakesh. Once in al-Andalus, they seized the region and incorporated it into their empire. The Almoravids ruled al-Andalus until 1146, when it was taken over by the Almohads, an even more conservative Muslim sect of Berber invaders.

It was into this world that Averroes was born in 1126. Politically and culturally, al-Andalus was experiencing upheaval. The tolerant society centered in Córdoba under the Umayyad caliphate was becoming a distant memory, as the Almoravids imposed a much more restrictive and austere view of Islam on the Andalusians. But even in this relatively repressive environment, Averroes would grow up around scholars, philosophers, theologians, jurists, and scientists—all searching for means of understanding the universe and the place of humans within it. From their works and teachings, Averroes would build an intellectual foundation upon which he could construct his own philosophy.

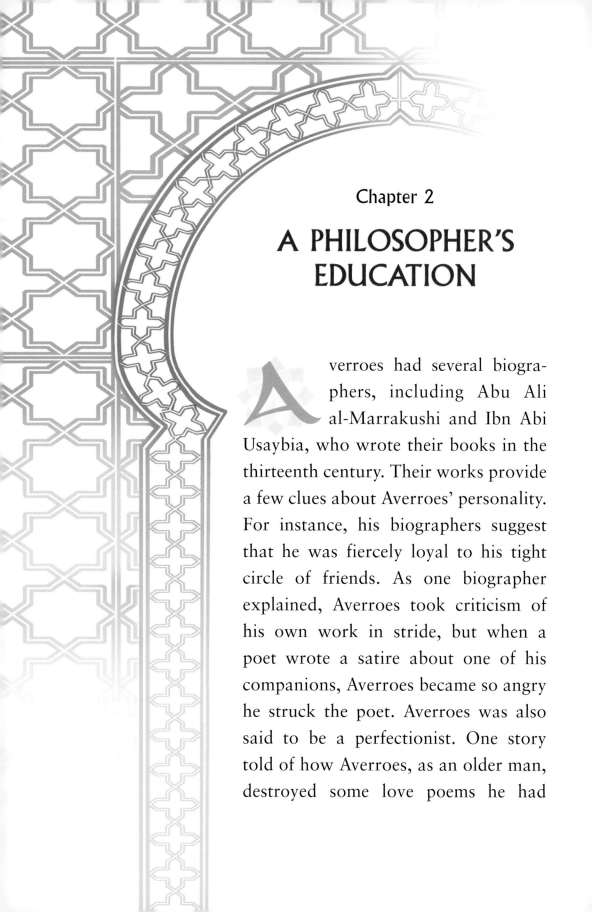

Chapter 2

A PHILOSOPHER'S EDUCATION

verroes had several biographers, including Abu Ali al-Marrakushi and Ibn Abi Usaybia, who wrote their books in the thirteenth century. Their works provide a few clues about Averroes' personality. For instance, his biographers suggest that he was fiercely loyal to his tight circle of friends. As one biographer explained, Averroes took criticism of his own work in stride, but when a poet wrote a satire about one of his companions, Averroes became so angry he struck the poet. Averroes was also said to be a perfectionist. One story told of how Averroes, as an older man, destroyed some love poems he had

The interior of the Great Mosque of Córdoba, also called La Mezquita, has many arcades of alternating red and white horseshoe-shaped arches. Construction of the Great Mosque was begun in 785 by Abd al-Rahman, who established the Umayyad dynasty in al-Andalus. Averroes' grandfather was the qadi and imam of La Mezquita.

composed in his youth, not because they were embarrassing, but because they were badly written. Averroes' biographers also portrayed him as an incredibly diligent scholar. One biographer noted that Averroes worked every night of his life, reading and writing, except for the day he got married and the day his father died.

THE MALIKI SCHOOL

None of Averroes' biographers, however, wrote about his earliest years. His family background, though, gives a sense of how he was raised and how he was educated. Averroes was born into one of the most important and influential families in al-Andalus. His father was a religious judge, or *qadi*. His grandfather was even more distinguished. He was the qadi and imam (a religious leader) of the Great Mosque of Córdoba, one of the city's most beautiful houses of worship. Given his lineage, Averroes was certainly schooled in Islamic law, so he would be qualified to follow in their footsteps.

Undoubtedly, Averroes' education included studying his grandfather's work. He was a follower of the Maliki school of Islamic law that originated in Medina in the eighth century. Its founder, Malik ibn Anas al-Asbahi (about 713–795), wrote *The Straight Path (Al-Muwatta)*, the earliest surviving book of Muslim laws. Averroes is said to have known *Al-Muwatta* by heart.

Averroes' grandfather took a relatively open-minded approach to the study of law. Some in the Maliki school did not think that humans should use reason to study the principles of law in the Qur'an. Averroes' grandfather, however, disagreed. As quoted in Roger Arnaldez's *Averroes: A Rationalist in Islam* (2000), Averroes' grandfather once wrote:

> God is known only through speculation regarding the signs of proof that He has made available in order that He might be known and that they might be used as proof. But only he who has reason capable of speculating and proving is able to speculate and carry out the proof.

MEDICINE AND SCIENCE

Averroes also was a student of medicine. One of his teachers was Abu Jafar ibn Harun al-Tarjali, a learned physician who was the personal doctor of an Almohad caliph. A contemporary of al-Tarjali's glowingly described al-Tarjali's talents as a physician and a scholar, according to Arnaldez's *Averroes*:

> He was among the most important inhabitants of Seville, an accomplished philosopher, established in this field, passionate about the works of Aristotle and other early philosophers, excellent and distinguished in the art of medicine, experienced in its foundations and applications, a good practitioner in the treatment of the ill, praiseworthy in the application of his methods.

A page from a 1217 Arabic translation of Galen's treatise on theriac (an antidote for poison) shows the physician Andromachus of the first century curing a man who has been bitten by a poisonous snake. As early as 850 the renowned physician Hunayn ibn Ishaq al-Ibadi of the court of Baghdad had listed 129 works by Galen to be translated from Greek to Arabic or Syriac for use by doctors and scholars. Averroes studied the Arabic translations of Galen's works and wrote many commentaries on them.

During his early medical studies, Averroes was certainly exposed to the work of the Greek physician Galen (about 129–199). Living in the second century, Galen was the most important medical writer in the ancient world. He wrote numerous treatises on anatomy, pharmacology, and diagnosis, as well as a work of philosophy, *On Medical Experience*.

Averroes was also interested in mathematics and science as a young man. He was particularly drawn to astronomy and probably was engaged in some scientific research in this area. Averroes once expressed regret that he did not have enough time to make a study of the movement of heavenly bodies. As he explained, according to Arnaldez in *Averroes*, "In my youth I was hoping that it would be possible to bring this research to fruition; but at the advanced age where I presently am, I have lost hope."

THE BEGINNINGS OF MUSLIM PHILOSOPHY

Growing up in the intellectually rich atmosphere of Córdoba, Averroes was undoubtedly educated in past and contemporary schools of Muslim philosophy, although none of his biographers lists his philosophy teachers by name. Philosophy—the study of the nature of reality and principles underlying thinking and being—originated in ancient Greece in the sixth century BC. Long before Averroes' birth, many of the most important works of Greek philosophy had been translated

The scholar al-Kindi is considered to be the first Muslim philosopher. He devoted most of his 300 books to the studies of philosophy and mathematics. His writings on Aristotle and his opinion that Greek philosophy was not in conflict with the Islamic faith greatly influenced Averroes' studies in Greek philosophy.

into Arabic in Baghdad, and these translated works had been imported to Córdoba. Also at Averroes' disposal were the writings of early Muslim philosophers, which contained their original ideas, as well as their thoughts on the works of the ancient Greeks, particularly Plato, Aristotle, and Plotinus.

The first Muslim scholar to embrace Greek philosophy was Yaqub ibn Ishaq al-Sabah al-Kindi (about 805–870). Producing more than 300 books, al-Kindi wrote on a wide range of subjects, including mathematics, logic, psychology, and astrology. But one of his most memorable works concentrated on the worth of studying Plato and Aristotle. Among

Socrates, Plato, and Aristotle

Philosophy in the Western world has been shaped in large part by three ancient Greeks—Socrates, Plato, and Aristotle.

Socrates (circa 470–399 BC) was a great teacher. In Athens, he taught his students by asking them questions, then asking more pointed questions based on the implications of their answers. This teaching method is now known as the Socratic method. Angering both religious and political leaders, Socrates was convicted of corrupting Athens's youth. He willingly accepted his sentence of death by drinking poison.

Socrates left behind no writings. His student Plato (about 427–347 BC) is responsible for recording what is known of his philosophy. Plato wrote and taught at the Academy, which he founded near Athens in 386. His writings were in the form of dialogues and covered a wide range of subjects, from law to mathematics. He argued that there were ideas, or forms, that had an independent reality and never changed. His best-known book is *The Republic*, which discusses the qualities of a just state.

Plato's most famous student was Aristotle (384–322 BC). Son of the physician to the Macedonian king, Aristotle became the tutor of Alexander the Great. In 335, Aristotle established a school, the Athenian Lyceum, which became one of the leading centers of learning in the ancient world. His philosophy concentrated on the systematic use of logic to discern unchanging principles that form the basis of all knowledge. Like Socrates, Aristotle faced criminal charges for teaching philosophy. He was forced to flee Athens to the city of Chalcis a year before his death.

This miniature of Socrates and his students is found in a Seljuk manuscript by al-Mubashshir entitled *Mukhtar al-Hikam* (*The Better Sentences and Most Precise Dictions,* also known as *Choice Maxims and Finest Sayings*) from the early thirteenth century. In the Socratic method of teaching, Socrates would pose a series of questions to expose the weaknesses of students' assumptions and to replace them with beliefs that seem closer to the truth. Plato was one of Socrates' students, and Aristotle was one of Plato's pupils. Averroes wrote commentaries on works by Plato and Aristotle.

his books was *The Quantity of the Books of Aristotle and What Is Required for the Acquisition of Philosophy.*

At the time, Muslim traditionalists were suspicious of Greek philosophy. They maintained that, as the work of pagans and foreigners, it provided nothing useful to the devout Muslim. Al-Kindi argued that the true seeker of truth had the duty to use whatever tools were available, "even if it were to come from distant races and nations different from us." Furthermore, al-Kindi claimed that Greek philosophy was not in conflict with the Islamic faith. On the contrary, he wrote that the tools of rational thought offered by the Greeks could actually be used to confirm the articles of faith revealed by the Qur'an.

THE NEOPLATONISTS

The development of Muslim philosophy was also shaped by Abu Nasr al-Farabi. Al-Farabi was the founder of Islamic Neoplatonism. Neoplatonism was a branch of philosophy that originated in Alexandria, an Egyptian city founded by Alexander the Great in 330 and captured by Arabs in 641. Neoplatonism was first developed by Plotinus, a Greek Egyptian philosopher who, during the third century AD, attempted to reconcile Greek philosophy with Eastern religious traditions.

The name Neoplatonism refers to Plato. But Plotinus's school of thought also drew from other Greek writers, including Aristotle and Pythagoras. It embraced elements of Judaism and Christianity as well. Neoplatonists believed that all existence came from a single source, the One, with which individual souls could be united spiritually.

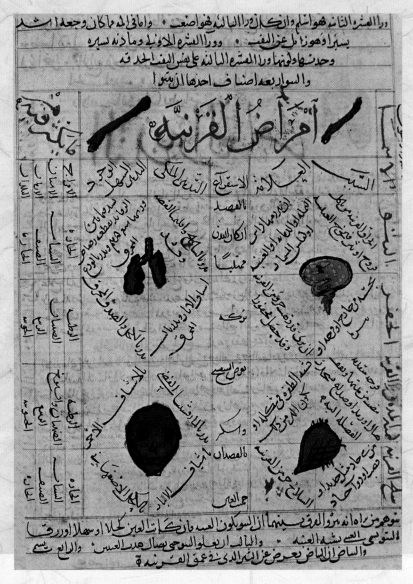

In the eleventh century, Avicenna (Ibn Sina) wrote *Canon of Medicine*, a multivolume text that combined medical knowledge from Greek, Roman, and Arab physicians and that served as a reference book for hundreds of years. The page pictured here is from a fourteenth-century copy of the *Canon* that shows information on the lungs, heart, brain, and skull.

For al-Farabi, the ultimate goal of humanity was to achieve happiness. He felt that happiness was not achievable in isolation, but possible only within the realm of human society. He envisioned an ideal state in which humans could find happiness. Because of these theories, al-Farabi is now considered the first Muslim political philosopher.

Before Averroes, the most important of the Muslim philosophers was Ibn Sina, better known in the West by his Latin name Avicenna. Born in Persia, Avicenna was considered a genius both in medicine and in philosophy. In his multivolume *Canon of Medicine,* he collected the medical knowledge of the Greeks, Arabs, and Romans, producing a text that would be consulted by physicians for centuries. As a philosopher, Avicenna was influenced by Neoplatonism, though his work concentrated on Aristotle. Like al-Farabi, Avicenna advanced an emanationist theory about the creation of the world, in which God was the starting point for a series of causes and effects that make up the structure of reality. Although in some respects his philosophy resembled al-Farabi's, Avicenna was a far more fluid writer, and his work reached a much larger readership.

Also central to Averroes' philosophical education was Ibn Bajjah, who was also known as Avempace. Avempace was the first major Muslim writer in al-Andalus to delve into philosophy. He wrote paraphrases of Aristotle's work and interpretations of al-Farabi's work, for whom he had great respect. Avempace paid a price for his intellectual adventures. Muslim traditionalists who opposed his writings had him imprisoned for heresy, or holding a belief contrary to accepted religious doctrine. He was freed only after Averroes' grandfather intervened.

INCOHERENCE OF THE PHILOSOPHERS

For many centuries, Muslim scholars had questioned whether philosophy could be reconciled with Muslim beliefs. But one of the most significant and sophisticated examinations of the matter was written a few decades before Averroes' birth by Abu Hamid al-Ghazali (about 1058–1111). A Persian, al-Ghazali was a learned theologian fully versed in the beliefs of the Neoplatonists, which he summarized in his book *Incoherence of the Philosophers*. His command of the subject made his ultimate attack on the Neoplatonism popularized by al-Farabi and Avicenna all the more devastating.

In *Incoherence of the Philosophers (Tahafut al-Falasifa)*, al-Ghazali conceded that some aspects of Greek Arab philosophy were useful paths to knowledge. He singled out logic and mathematics, since he did not see them in conflict with religious truth. But al-Ghazali condemned metaphysics—the branch of philosophy that deals with the nature of reality— as wholly incompatible with Islam. He argued that the

In *Incoherence of the Philosophers (Tahafut al-Falasifa)*, al-Ghazali, depicted here in a modern-day painting, wrote that he did not see logic and mathematics conflicting with Islamic teachings. He did find, however, that metaphysics was contrary to Islam. He also condemned the Neoplatonists for challenging the transcendence of God. Averroes undoubtedly studied al-Ghazali's book.

Qur'an presents an all-powerful God, without whom man is nothing. Al-Ghazali condemned the Neoplatonists for challenging the transcendence of God by subjecting him to categories of human thought.

Al-Ghazali's book was a landmark in Muslim thought. In large part because of *Incoherence of the Philosophers*, the study of Greek philosophy fell out of favor in the western portions of the Muslim Empire. Almost certainly, Averroes read it as part of his early education.

AN INFLUENTIAL MENTOR

Of Averroes' contemporaries, the philosopher who had the most influence on Averroes was Abu Bakr ibn Tufayl. Ibn Tufayl helped revive Neoplatonism in Muslim Spain through his book *Living Son of the Awake (Risalat Hayy ibn Yaqzan)*, a philosophical novel. It told the story of a man trapped alone on a desert island. Through observation and thought, Ibn Tufayl's character was able to discover truths about God and the world.

However, to Ibn Tufayl, philosophical contemplation ultimately fell short. He believed a soul could not be united with the One God without a mystical emptying out of the self.

As an adult, Averroes was friendly with Ibn Tufayl, although he had little sympathy for the mystical aspects of his philosophy. Ibn Tufayl's great influence over Averroes' life did not come from his work but from his connections. It was Ibn Tufayl who introduced Averroes to his patron, the caliph Abu Yaqub Yusuf, thus setting in motion Averroes' brilliant career in philosophy.

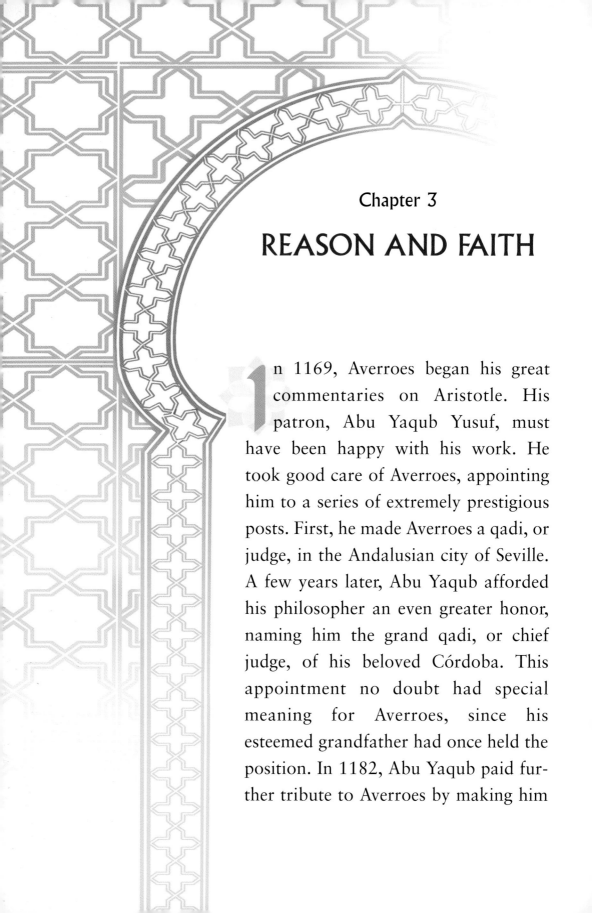

Chapter 3

REASON AND FAITH

In 1169, Averroes began his great commentaries on Aristotle. His patron, Abu Yaqub Yusuf, must have been happy with his work. He took good care of Averroes, appointing him to a series of extremely prestigious posts. First, he made Averroes a qadi, or judge, in the Andalusian city of Seville. A few years later, Abu Yaqub afforded his philosopher an even greater honor, naming him the grand qadi, or chief judge, of his beloved Córdoba. This appointment no doubt had special meaning for Averroes, since his esteemed grandfather had once held the position. In 1182, Abu Yaqub paid further tribute to Averroes by making him

Aristotle is considered to be one of the three greatest intellects in ancient Greek philosophy (the other two being Socrates and Plato). Aristotle's thinking encompassed a vast array of subjects, including biology, zoology, chemistry, physics, psychology, political theory, logic, ethics, metaphysics, and history. Averroes continued the immense task of writing commentaries on Aristotle's works while he served as a judge and doctor.

his personal physician, a position previously held by Averroes' friend and mentor Ibn Tufayl.

These years were busy for Averroes, as he often traveled between Marrakesh, Córdoba, and Seville in order to fulfill his official duties as a judge and physician. But, despite his active public life, he was also engulfed in the private world of scholarship. His work on Aristotle was a massive endeavor, but he continued to write on a wide variety of other topics. Some of his most important works at this time were his books about theology, in which he made a passionate, rational

Aristotle's treatises on logic are referred to collectively as *Organon* (fourth century BC). This manuscript page is from an eleventh-century Arabic translation of Aristotle's *Organon*. Averroes wrote short commentaries on Aristotle's treatises on *Poetics*, *Rhetoric*, and *Topics*, which were included in the *Organon* collection.

argument for the essential compatibility of Aristotelian philosophy and Muslim thought.

ARISTOTLE'S PHILOSOPHY

Born in 384 BC, Aristotle was an influential thinker even in his day. For twenty years, he studied with Plato, the greatest Greek philosopher before Aristotle. Plato taught that true knowledge, an understanding of the essence of things, could only come to the contemplative soul who turns away from the world. Driven by an overriding interest in understanding the material world around him, Aristotle in contrast valued the knowledge humans could obtain by using their senses.

Aristotle proposed an ordered, systematic study of the world, creating categories of study, such as biology and physics, that continue to be used by scholars today. His own writings about the natural world included *Physics*, *Meteorology*, and *History of Animals*. In general, Aristotle had an enormous impact on all sciences by encouraging the idea of expanding scientific knowledge through direct observation. Aristotle also wrote about the art of public speaking in *Rhetoric* and analyzed literature in *Poetics*.

In the field of philosophy, one of Aristotle's greatest contributions was a system of reasoning called logic. In fact, in Muslim lands, Aristotle was often called Sahib al-Mantiq, Arabic for "Master of Logic." Central to Aristotle's system

In this French drawing from the thirteenth century, Averroes *(left)* is portrayed speaking with Porphyry (circa 232–304), the Greek scholar and Neoplatonic philosopher. Porphyry wrote *Isagoge*, an introduction to the logic of Aristotle that became the prevailing reference book for centuries. Averroes wrote a middle-length commentary on Porphyry's *Isagoge*.

of logical reasoning was the syllogism. In a syllogism, two statements, called premises, logically lead to a third, known as a conclusion. For instance, Aristotle himself provided this example: if all humans are mortal and all Greeks are humans, then all Greeks are mortal.

In his *Metaphysics*, Aristotle presented his theory of the nature of reality. In a departure from Plato, Aristotle insisted that the study of metaphysics must begin in an investigation of what humans could learn from their senses, then move from that point to abstract thought. In this work, Aristotle also presented God as the highest form of being, pure intelligence without material form. Aristotle thought the world had always existed, just as God had always existed. The world was neither created nor consciously controlled by God, who did not affect day-to-day events. Aristotle also held that humans were the only creatures with an intelligence resembling that of God's. It was, therefore, man's highest calling to devote himself to reasoned thought.

WRITING THE COMMENTARIES

Averroes approached Aristotle's works by writing commentaries in three different lengths—short, medium, and long. The short commentaries were little more than paraphrases of the originals. The long commentaries were lengthy scholarly discourses, often devoting pages to explain a short passage. Some later writers dismissed Averroes' work as just slavish rewordings of Aristotle's writings. But Averroes' most sophisticated commentaries were truly original works. While illuminating Aristotle's thinking, they also provided unique interpretations that give us a view into Averroes' own personal philosophical beliefs.

Interpreting Aristotle's teachings was certainly a formidable task. As Averroes' patron, Abu Yaqub Yusuf had discovered,

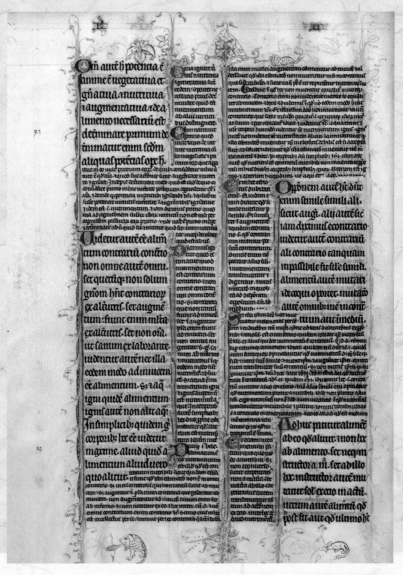

These two manuscript pages from the thirteenth century are Latin translations of Aristotle's *De Anima* (On the Soul) with Averroes' commentaries appearing in the middle columns of the pages. In this work, Averroes' notes take precedence over Aristotle's text, which is relegated to the outer columns.

182

Aristotle was a complex thinker whose meaning was often hard to discern. About thirty works of Aristotle survive, which amount to less than a quarter of the writings he produced. Many of the extant writings are not polished works meant for publication. They were probably lecture notes. Not surprisingly, some passages in these works are highly repetitive, while the language in others is confoundingly terse or obscure. The material was probably put in sequence by ancient editors rather than by Aristotle himself, making them all the more confusing.

In interpreting Aristotle, Averroes faced an additional obstacle—the translations with which he had to work. Averroes did not study Aristotle's original Greek texts, but instead he worked from Arabic versions. Their translators had an imperfect knowledge of the ancient Greek language. As a result, the Arabic translations were often at best muddled and at worst outright inaccurate. In making his commentaries, Averroes constantly had to compare the various translations to which he had access. For many passages, he had to decide which translation seemed the most reliable. His writings often alluded to choices he had had to make and offered justifications for them.

Averroes faced still another challenge in his commentaries. A number of Arabic translations wrongly attributed to Aristotle's works were in fact written by two later Greek philosophers, Plotinus and Proclus, both proponents of

Averroes and Plato

Aristotle wrote a treatise titled *Politics*, which is now one of his most widely read works. Averroes, however, never wrote a commentary on this book because, in his words, "[It] has not fallen into our hands." It was the only major work of Aristotle's that was not translated into Arabic in Averroes' lifetime. Averroes, though, was able to paraphrase another great discussion of politics from the ancient world—*The Republic* by Plato.

Plato's *Republic* dealt with the question of what justice is and how people should be governed. In it, Plato explained his notion of the ideal government, which would be ruled by a philosopher king. *The Republic* also presented the theory that human society could change and even be perfected.

In Averroes' world, many of the ideas in *The Republic* were considered controversial, if not dangerous. The rulers of al-Andalus did not want average people to wonder if their government could be improved. And they certainly did not want people to ponder whether the social order that placed the rulers at the top was something that could be changed.

Neoplatonism. One of Averroes' goals was in essence to purify the Muslim texts of Aristotelian philosophy by sorting out those ideas that were genuinely Aristotle's from those inserted into his work by later thinkers. By repeatedly pointing out passages that he believed were inconsistent with

Aristotle's core beliefs, Averroes hoped to present a truer version of Aristotle's philosophy than had previously been available in Muslim lands.

INCOHERENCE OF THE INCOHERENCE

The influence of Aristotle is evident in much of Averroes' other writings, including his works about Islamic theology. These included *Decisive Treatise on the Relation of Philosophy and Religion* and *Exposition of the Methods of Proof*. His best-known religious work, however, was *Incoherence of the Incoherence*.

The title was a clever play on *Incoherence of the Philosophers*, written by the famous Muslim theologian Abu Hamid al-Ghazali. Al-Ghazali's book had a deep influence on Muslim thought with its devastating critique of philosophy. He argued that philosophy presented theories that were fundamentally at odds with Islamic principles by meticulously examining twenty questions discussed by the philosophers. Al-Ghazali then concluded that, for a devout Muslim, the philosophers' answers to some of these questions amounted to heresy.

A large element of al-Ghazali's attack was his insistence that even if philosophy did not contradict Islam, as a system of thought it was so incoherent that it was utterly useless as a tool for studying the world. While making this argument, al-Ghazali hoped to destroy the influence of al-Farabi and Avicenna. At the time the book was written, they were the leading Muslim proponents of the philosophy of the ancient Greeks.

Just as al-Ghazali's *Incoherence of the Philosophers* was a direct attack on al-Farabi and Avicenna, Averroes' *Incoherence* was meant to be a direct attack on al-Ghazali. Averroes took on al-Ghazali point by point, offering a thorough defense of Aristotle. Averroes condemned al-Ghazali for denouncing philosophy, which he celebrated as a valid and valuable means for examining God and the world.

In writing *Incoherence*, Averroes had another goal as well. He wanted his readership to reexamine the work of Avicenna and other earlier Muslim philosophers, whom he believed had misunderstood Aristotle. This was in part because they blindly followed the flawed Arabic translations containing elements of Neoplatonist beliefs. Just as in his commentaries, Averroes wanted to purify Aristotle from outside influences; in *Incoherence* he wanted to purify Muslim philosophy from ideas that misrepresented Aristotle's work.

THE ORIGIN OF THE WORLD

One of Averroes' central arguments with al-Ghazali dealt with the origin of the world. According to al-Ghazali, Aristotle

والحمد لله وحده وصلى الله على محمد وعلى آله ● وبعد
حمداً لله الواجب والصلاة على جميع رسله وانبيائه
فان اغرضي في هذا القول ان نبين مراتب الاقاويل الثبتة
في كتبها ايها منها في التصديق ولا اقناع وقصور اكثرها
عن مرتبة اليقين والبرهان قال ابوحامد حكاية الادلة
الفلاسفة في قدم العالم ولنقتصر من ادلتهم في هذا
الفن على ما له موقع في النفس قال وهذا الفن من الادلة
هو ثلاثة اوجه الدليل الاول قولهم يستحيل صدق
حادث من قديم مطلق لانا اذا افرضنا القديم ولم يصدر
منه لعله المثل لم يصدق فانما المتصدد لانه لم يكن للوجود
مرجح بل لوجود العالم يكن عنه امكان صرفاً فاذا احدث بعد
ذلك بعد ان لم يكن اما ان يتجدد مرجح او لا يتجدد فان لم يتجدد
مرجح بقي العالم على الامكان الصرف كما كان قبل ذلك
وان تجدد مرجح انتقل الكلام الى ذلك المرجح لم يرجح
الآن ولم يرجح قبل فاما ان يبرز الامر الى غير النهاية اوينتهى الى
مرجح لم يزل مرجحاً قلت هذا القول هو يجري على مراتب
الجدل وليس هو واصلاً موصل البراهين لانه مقدماته
موصل

This page is from an eighteenth-century copy of Averroes'
Incoherence of the Incoherence (*Tahafut al-Tahafut*, 1184). In his book,
Averroes refuted al-Ghazali's *Incoherence of the Philosophers* and reex-
amined Muslim philosophers' works that he believed misrepresented
Aristotle's writings.

maintained that the world was eternal. For Aristotle, there could not have been a time when God existed but the world did not, since time is a measure of changing events, and there could be no changing events without the world.

Al-Ghazali devoted much of his book to the question of the world's origin. He claimed that the philosopher's view contradicted Islam because several passages of the Qur'an suggest that God created the world. In the traditional Muslim view, the world was created *ex nihilo* (that is, out of nothing) and was kept in existence only through God's will and power.

Averroes felt that al-Ghazali misrepresented Aristotle, whose beliefs, in his eyes, were actually entirely reconcilable with the Qur'an. According to Averroes' interpretation, the philosopher believed the world was neither eternal nor created in time, but that it was created from eternity. He attacked al-Ghazali's contention that creation could have occurred in time because it brought into question God's omnipotence. If God were all-powerful, how could there have been a time before which he could not create the world? And if he could create it at any time, why would he have chosen the time he did?

WHAT GOD KNOWS

Aristotle argued that God can only think "of what is most divine and precious." He maintained it was unworthy of

God to know of mundane matters, asking, "Are there not some things about which it is incredible that it [God] should think?" To al-Ghazali, this belief meant that God's knowledge was limited. Anyone who believed this, therefore, was a heretic, since it contradicts the Qur'anic view that God's knowledge is unlimited.

Similarly, al-Ghazali spoke out against Aristotle's contention that God did not play a role in day-to-day affairs of the world. He explained that, to human beings, there may seem to be a consistent and unalterable pattern of causes that create certain effects, but God, being all-powerful, could change that at any time. Al-Ghazali argued that, in fact, the Qur'an reports of just this kind of intervention in its description of miracles. For instance, people expect for an object that comes into contact with fire to burn. But the Qur'an recounted that when Abraham's enemies tried to kill him by setting him aflame, the fire did not burn him. In this case, God intervened in the world in a way that altered the expected pattern of cause and effect.

For Averroes, al-Ghazali's criticism boiled the argument down to whether God knows only universal truths or knows all particulars of life on earth. Averroes argued that this discussion was fundamentally flawed because it made the mistake of comparing God's knowledge to human knowledge. He said that divine knowledge and human knowledge have to be radically different. Human knowledge, after all, comes from examining the effect of a thing known. Divine knowledge, on the other hand, is the cause of the thing known. To Averroes, it is part of God's mystery that human beings cannot understand divine knowledge.

THE AFTERLIFE

In al-Ghazali's opinion, the nature of the afterlife was another area in which philosophy was in conflict with Islam. Since the Islamic concept of the afterlife included bodily sensations, al-Ghazali maintained that scripture made it clear that the soul was reunited with the body after death, contrary to the philosophers' denial of bodily resurrection. He asked, "What is the objection to admitting the conjunction of both spiritual and bodily pleasures as well as corresponding miseries?"

Averroes was not troubled by this apparent conflict. He suggested that the afterlife depicted in the Qur'an was intended to impress upon common people the necessity of living good lives. Averroes believed that only a small number of people were capable of choosing to live correctly merely because it was the right thing to do. Everyone else required the lure of eternal rewards or the threat of eternal punishment.

Averroes pointed out that the Qur'an itself acknowledges that it should be read on different levels. In several

The ascension of Muhammad is portrayed in this sixteenth-century Persian manuscript, *Khamsa* (The Quintet), written by the epic poet Nizami (circa 1141–1209). Al-Ghazali believed that Islamic teachings about the afterlife were in conflict with the study of philosophy because Muslims believed that the soul was reunited with the body after death. Most Greek philosophers, on the other hand, did not believe that the physical body was resurrected after death.

passages, the Qur'an notes that most of its verses are easily understood. These constitute the core of the scriptures that every Muslim can comprehend. But the Qur'an itself also declares that some of its verses are ambiguous, thus open to interpretation. According to Averroes, only those "well-grounded in knowledge" could truly understand these difficult verses. And for Averroes, no one could be well-grounded in knowledge without an understanding of philosophy. In his view, not only was the study of philosophy compatible with Islam, but the Qur'an actually encouraged its use.

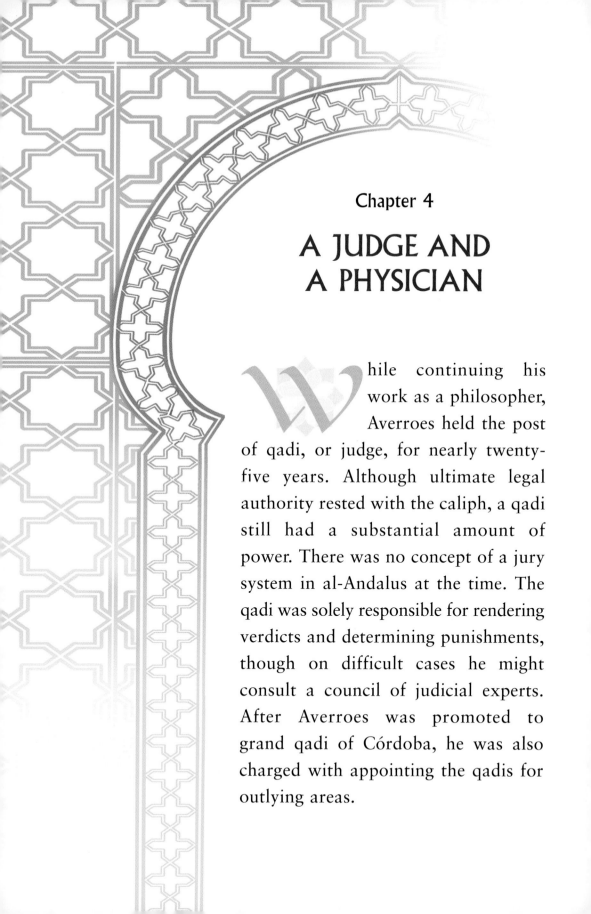

Chapter 4

A JUDGE AND A PHYSICIAN

While continuing his work as a philosopher, Averroes held the post of qadi, or judge, for nearly twenty-five years. Although ultimate legal authority rested with the caliph, a qadi still had a substantial amount of power. There was no concept of a jury system in al-Andalus at the time. The qadi was solely responsible for rendering verdicts and determining punishments, though on difficult cases he might consult a council of judicial experts. After Averroes was promoted to grand qadi of Córdoba, he was also charged with appointing the qadis for outlying areas.

This fifteenth-century miniature of a pilgrim encampment in Mecca is from a treatise on the law of religious observances by the jurist and theologian Abu Hanifah (699–767). The Hanafi school of law, one of the four canonical schools of Islamic jurisprudence (the other three being the Shafi, Maliki, and Hanbali), was the most liberal of all the schools. It put less emphasis on oral traditions and more on reason and personal judgment.

THE SHARIA

Despite their considerable authority, the qadis had restrictions on their legal decisions. They had to apply the sharia, or religious law. The sharia is composed of laws that involve divine revelation. These include about 350 verses scattered throughout the Qur'an that deal with legal issues. The law is also found in the Sunna (custom). (The Sunna is also a source for developing law.) This is a body of teachings, recorded by Muhammad's early followers, based on things the Prophet said and did. For a qadi, the rules set out in the Qur'an and Sunna had to be weighed carefully, since the former is considered the word of God, and the latter is considered the custom of the Prophet.

The Qur'an and the Sunna do not deal with every possible legal problem that could arise. For the issues they do not address directly, the qadi turned to *fiqh* to further develop the law. Fiqh was the process by which the Qur'an and Sunna could be interpreted to create law. Fiqh did not have the same authority as the Qur'an because it was the work of humans, not God.

The proper application of Islamic law was long the subject of debate among scholars. By the time Averroes became a qadi, several different schools of law had emerged. The Hanafi school allowed judges some room to interpret law based on the use of specific intellectual tools. For instance, if the sharia did not apply directly to a specific case, a Hanafi qadi could make a ruling based on custom or even on his own judicial preference.

Averroes was trained in the Maliki school, which was more conservative. But it still allowed qadis some flexibility. A Maliki qadi was permitted, for example, to consider the public interest in deciding a case. He could also make a ruling in order to "block the means." This meant a qadi could prevent someone brought before the court from performing a lawful act if the qadi believed it would ultimately lead to illegal behavior.

A MALIKI PRIMER

Averroes wrote several treatises about Islamic law. The most extensive was *Primer of the Discretionary Scholar (Bidayat al-Mujtahid)*. The *Primer*, which he wrote in 1168, summarized the history of the different schools of Islamic law and discussed why they each came to the conclusions they did. Unlike his writings on philosophy and theology, this work represented fairly traditional ideas. (Some scholars have even suggested that it is so conventional it could not actually have been written by Averroes.)

In the *Primer*, Averroes acknowledged the complete authority of the sharia. He also generally supported the Maliki point of view, although he occasionally expressed opinions at variance with it. For instance, Averroes' writing strongly stressed the need for legal interpretation through

In his *Primer of the Discretionary Scholar (Bidayat al-Mujtahid)*, the cover of which a 1987 facsimile edition is pictured, Averroes analyzed Islamic jurisprudence. This 1168 work is considered by many scholars to be the best discussion on the Maliki school of fiqh.

reasoning. He was especially an advocate for the use of analogy, a reasoning tool first promoted by the Hanafi school. Averroes held that when there was no law from the sharia that addressed a specific case, a qadi could rule based on a law that dealt with a matter that was similar, or analogous, to the case at hand.

One biographer of Averroes described a case he ruled on by using analogous reasoning. The students of a male professor began gossiping that their teacher was having a romantic relationship with a handsome young man. One student even wrote a poem about the affair. As it turned out, the gossip was untrue, and the professor approached Averroes, asking him to punish the students who had spread the story. Since homosexual acts were against Muslim law, the professor claimed they had falsely accused him of a crime.

To make his judgment, Averroes referred to a story in the Qur'an. It told of a chaste woman who was falsely accused of a shameful act. Her accusers were punished by eighty blows from a whip. Although this case involved a wrongly accused woman instead of a wrongly accused man, Averroes found they were similar enough to justify ruling against the professor's accusers. The biographer did not record the exact punishment Averroes ordered.

For readers of his philosophical works, Averroes' defense for using analogy in legal proceedings was familiar. In some instances, Averroes felt judges could use reasoning to settle legal disputes just as he believed that seekers of truth could use reasoning to solve theological or philosophical questions.

PHYSICIAN TO THE CALIPH

In 1182, Averroes began a third career, with his appointment as the physician to the royal court in Marrakesh. The appointment was undoubtedly a great honor. But it is not clear how much hands-on work was involved. There is no record of Averroes having been a practicing physician before his appointment. However, it is still obvious from his writings that he had an extensive background in medicine—knowledge that probably was sufficient to provide medical treatment to the caliph and his court.

In Averroes' day, there was an extensive body of medical works available in al-Andalus. Much of the information was handed down from the ancient Greeks, particularly the philosopher and physician Galen. Averroes himself produced about twenty books about medicine, most written before he became court physician. The majority were summaries and paraphrases of Galen dealing with a wide variety of topics,

A sixteenth-century Arabic copy of Averroes' commentary on Avicenna's *Poem on Medicine* shows Averroes' prose commentary written in red ink and Avicenna's text written in black ink. Avicenna's poem, which contained 1,326 verses, was the subject of many commentaries, but Averroes' was the most well known.

الى موضعه يرده يتولد رطب الخلاع الحاصل الفاصل هو بان يمد كل واحد من العضوين الى اجنبهما المتقابلتين ثم تهمل عنهما حتى يدخلا جميعا هو وافق الاخر اعني المفصل في ذي المفصل وبعد ما كان لم يؤد ان آله معروف يعرف ذلك تسهله وحبس اعتداد وبعد ما نرده الشده تترك ذلك مرها مما تعده يلزمه من الدوا واتابعها تطعيم من الطعام ما امضا حتى يزوا سالما ورم ولايجاب الاجتماع من دم اقل ما تبربه بعد شهر وربما يتم ذلك اكثر وقد فرغت من جميع العمل ولان النظم بعود محكم بيعود وبعد ما يرجع العضو الى مفصله تتركه زمانا محرد راحتي يسلم من الورم ثلاثة ايام بان يحمل عليه الادوية النابضه حتى يسلم بذلك من التوم ثم يلزم صاحبه تسكين ذلك العضو لاقل من شهر وربما الحتجن ان يبقى عشر ابعد الشهر اعني اربعين يوما وهنا القضى التولد في شرح من الارجوزه حمد الله وعونه ووافق الفراغ منها يوم الاربعاني من شعبان سنة ثلاث وثلاثين وستمايه للهجري النبويه وصلى الله على سيدنا محمد سيد الرسلين دعلى اله واصحابه الطيبين كانه وسلم تسليما كثيرا و هو حساد نعم الوكيل ووافق الفراغ من هذه النسخة المباركه يوم الاربعا ساد سر عشر التعده الحرام من شهور سنة خمسة والفمس الهجري النبويه على صاحبها انخل الصلاه والسلام و غوننه لكاتبها والديه ولمن طالع في هذا الكتاب والله الوكيل اللهم آمين آمين

Advice from the Medical Expert

Throughout *Generalities in Medicine*, Averroes offers practical advice about how to maintain one's health. He is especially generous with dietary advice, some of which sounds as though it could have been written by a nutritionist today. In this excerpt from Caroline Stone's 2003 article entitled "Doctor, Philosopher, Renaissance Man," Averroes extols the healthful benefits of cooking with olive oil:

> When [oil] comes from ripe, healthy olives and its properties have not been tempered with artificially, it can be assimilated perfectly by the human body. Food seasoned with olive oil is nutritious, provided the oil is fresh and not rancid. Generally speaking, all olive oil is excellent for people and for that reason in [al-Andalus] it is the only medium needed for cooking meat, given that the best way of preparing it is what we call braising. This is how it is done: Take oil and pour it in a cooking pot. Place the meat in it and then add hot water, a little at a time, simmering it without letting it boil.

from fevers to medications to hygiene. Averroes also wrote a commentary on *Poem on Medicine (Al-Urjuzah fi al-Tib)*, a medical poem written by Avicenna.

However, Averroes' best-known medical work was *Generalities in Medicine (Al-Kulliyyat*, written between 1153 and 1169). In the twelfth century, it was translated into Latin and given the title *Colliget*. In this form, Averroes' work was used as a medical textbook in Europe for centuries.

GENERALITIES IN MEDICINE

As the title suggests, *Generalities* was intended to provide physicians with general principles that governed the body in illness and in health. One of Averroes' biographers, Ibn Abi Usaybia, noted that the book was conceived as one part of a two-volume set. According to Arnaldez's *Averroes*, Ibn Abi Usaybia wrote, "Averroes composed his book on generalities and asked Avenzoar, to write his on particularities, so that, together, their two books would form a perfect work on the art of medicine." A friend of Averroes', Avenzoar (also known as Ibn Zuhr) had conducted medical experiments and probably had more experience dealing directly with patients. Averroes perhaps thought Avenzoar was a better choice than himself to tackle the "particularities" of medicine, that is, the day-to-day care of the human body.

Arnaldez quotes the end of *Generalities*, where Averroes wrote "He who has mastered the generalities that we have written will be able to understand what is correct and what is erroneous in the therapeutic practice of the authors of kunnash [works of therapy]." But his book provided more than just guidelines for judging specific medicinal treatments. It also gave readers plenty of practical advice. It

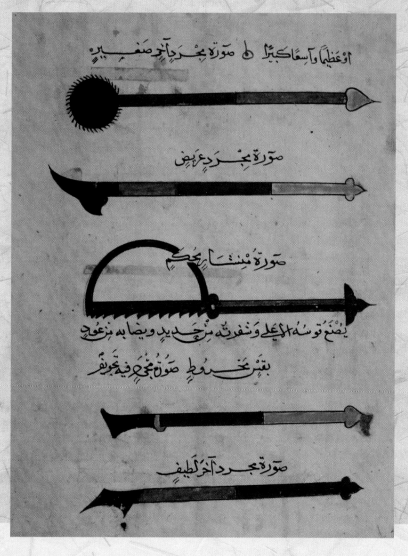

Albucasis (Abu al-Qasim) is considered to be one of the greatest surgeons of the Middle Ages. Albucasis (circa 936–1013), who was born near Córdoba, wrote a comprehensive text on surgical procedures and instruments, entitled *An Aid to Him Who Lacks the Capacity to Read Big Books (Al-Tasrif li man ajaz an-il-talif)*, usually called *The Method of Medicine*. These drawings of surgical instruments are from a twelfth-century copy of Albucasis's manuscript. Averroes explained and expanded on many medical writings, including those of Albucasis and Avicenna.

systematically discussed the body, recounting the proper workings of its various parts, how they could be affected by illness, and how these illnesses could be treated.

In keeping with the Muslim medical beliefs of his day, Averroes placed a great emphasis on keeping the body well. In fact, he defined medicine as "an effective art, based on true principles and concerned with preserving man's health and abating disease, as far as possible." Accordingly, his books often gave detailed advice about everyday matters such as nutrition and physical activity. In one work, he counseled readers to eat a balanced diet of bread, poultry, fish, and mutton, though he cautioned against eating any fruits but figs and grapes. He advised that regular exercise should take place after a meal and be followed by bathing. Averroes also maintained that in restoring health, natural methods, such as changes in diet, were generally more effective than artificial means, such as medicine and surgery. Averroes wrote:

> When the physician treats a patient in any way at all, he is really assisting nature according to a determinate course of action and towards a determinate goal . . . If the physician is ignorant of that course or that goal . . . and treats the patient in a haphazard way, he will be essentially at fault and is right only by accident.

In general, Averroes' writings on medicine and health were the least original of his works. He drew heavily on

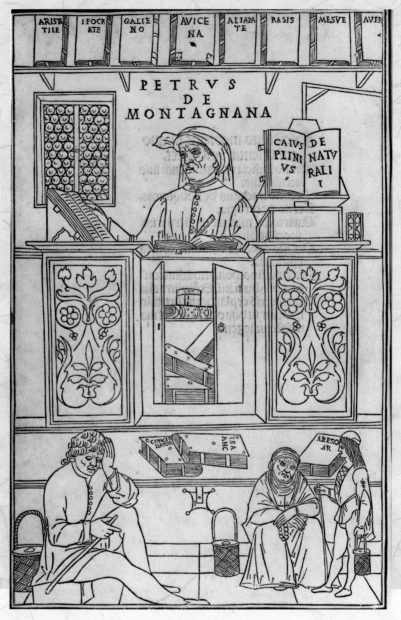

This engraving of Pietro da Montagnana shows the Paduan medical teacher surrounded by landmark medical texts that were written by Greek and Muslim physicians and scholars, including Aristotle, Hippocrates, Galen, Avicenna, al-Razi, Avenzoar, and Averroes *(top, right)*, while patients in the foreground await examinations. The illustration was printed in Johannes de Ketham's *Fasciculus Medicinae* (1495), a medical book that pays tribute to the Muslim influence on Western medicine.

existing medical texts, including Avicenna's famous *Canon of Medicine*, which covered a much wider breadth of knowledge than Averroes' *Generalities*. Averroes, though, did contribute to medical science by his insistence that a physician had to use reason to diagnose illness and determine a course of treatment. Like Galen and Avicenna, Averroes held that one could not be a good physician without also being a good philosopher.

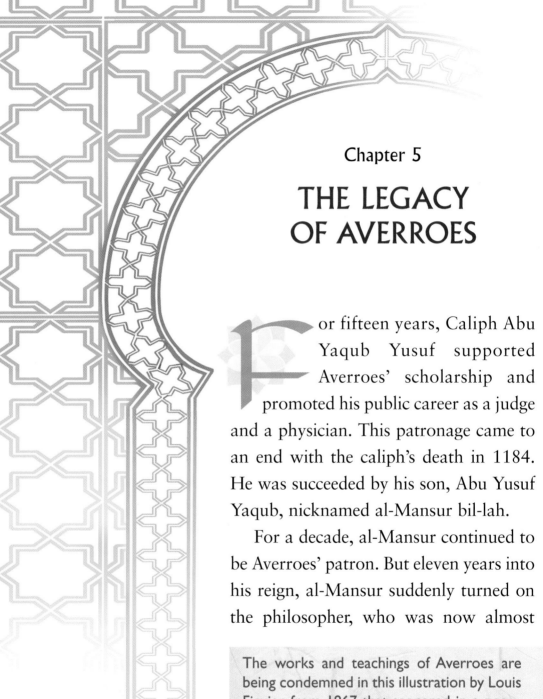

Chapter 5

THE LEGACY OF AVERROES

For fifteen years, Caliph Abu Yaqub Yusuf supported Averroes' scholarship and promoted his public career as a judge and a physician. This patronage came to an end with the caliph's death in 1184. He was succeeded by his son, Abu Yusuf Yaqub, nicknamed al-Mansur bil-lah.

For a decade, al-Mansur continued to be Averroes' patron. But eleven years into his reign, al-Mansur suddenly turned on the philosopher, who was now almost

The works and teachings of Averroes are being condemned in this illustration by Louis Figuier from 1867 that appeared in a popular French book about the lives of learned men of the Middle Ages. Al-Mansur, the caliph, banished Averroes from Marrakesh in 1195 and ordered that his books be burned. Today, no one knows for certain the reason for the caliph's and Averroes' falling-out.

seventy years old. The caliph banished both Averroes and his followers from the court. Furthermore, Averroes was forbidden to write about philosophy, politics, and religion, and many of his books were burned.

BANISHED

It is not certain exactly what happened between Averroes and al-Mansur. Biographer Ibn Abi Usaybia speculated that Averroes had offended al-Mansur by referring to him in print as the king of the Berbers, since "Berbers" in Arabic could be used to mean "barbarians."

More likely, though, politics played the biggest role in the caliph's attack on Averroes. At the time, al-Mansur was battling Christians in what is now known as Spain and was desperate for the support of Maliki judges, who still held great sway among the people. Even though Averroes himself was a Maliki qadi, more conservative judges held him in suspicion because of his embrace of philosophy and philosophers. In fact, records suggest that some enemies of philosophy were calling for Averroes to be put to death.

In the end, Averroes' punishment was far less severe. After his banishment, he was probably confined to a home in al-Isalah (now Lucena) near Córdoba in a fairly comfortable version of house arrest. Nevertheless, Averroes' banishment must have been a painful experience. His personal reputation was sullied, and he was publicly branded as a bad Muslim. At least once during his exile, he was chased away from a Córdoba mosque by a furious mob.

After two years, the caliph recalled Averroes to Marrakesh. The ban on Averroes' writings was also lifted, although it appears that the elderly philosopher wrote nothing after returning to the Almohad capital. Averroes remained in the caliph's good graces until his death on December 11, 1198. Three months later, in accordance with his wishes, his body was laid to rest in Córdoba. According to Caroline Stone's article, "Doctor, Philosopher, Renaissance Man," an eyewitness wrote about Averroes' funeral:

> When the coffin with his body was laid upon the bier [coffin stand], they put his works on the opposite side to serve as a counterweight. I was standing there . . . and I said to myself, "On one side the master and on the other his works."

THE END OF AL-ANDALUS

Averroes' many friends and associates mourned his passing. But in the years following his death, his reputation suffered in Muslim lands. Some scholars denigrated his work, perhaps none as pointedly as the philosopher Ibn Sabin. Dismissing Averroes as "merely an imitator of Aristotle," Ibn Sabin wrote that "he was a man of limited scope, faint understanding, foolish conceptions and lacking in intuition."

The conquest of Granada by the Catholic monarchs Ferdinand and Isabella in 1492 ended the reign of the Nasrids, the last Muslim rulers in al-Andalus. This fifteenth-century relief of the battle is from a choir stall in Toledo Cathedral, in Castile, Spain. After Averroes' death, his reputation suffered and his works were criticized. As al-Andalus's power in Muslim lands diminished, so did Averroes' acclaim.

More commonly, though, Averroes' writings were merely ignored by Muslim scholars. After Averroes' death, philosophy in general fell into disrepute among Muslims. Averroes may have laid a foundation for Muslim philosophy in al-Andalus, but in subsequent years, no one bothered to

build upon it. Interest in theology, however, continued to grow. While Averroes' work was largely dismissed, the writings of his old rival, al-Ghazali, grew in stature. Even to this day, al-Ghazali remains an important figure in Muslim thought.

This fifteenth-century manuscript from Saragossa, Spain, is a Hebrew copy of Averroes' commentary on Aristotle's treatise *On Generation and Corruption*. The original Hebrew manuscript of Averroes' commentary was commissioned by a Jew, Don Judah ibn Lavi de la Cavalleria, who became the royal treasurer for King James of Aragon in 1257.

In the decades following Averroes' death, al-Andalus itself was waning in power. The great culture once centered in Córdoba disintegrated after many years of political turmoil. By the 1270s, Muslim Spain had been reduced to a small area around the city of Granada. (By this time, the Abbasid caliphate based in Baghdad had also come to an end. The Abbasids, long in decline, lost all power in 1258, when their capital was overrun by invading tribes of Mongols from central Asia.)

But ironically, as al-Andalus was fading away, its influence over its European neighbors was beginning to grow. Leaving the dying city, scholars from al-Andalus began to scatter throughout Europe. With them, they brought new ideas and books, which eventually made their way to cities such as Paris, France; Bologna, Italy; and Oxford, England.

PHILOSOPHY IN EUROPE

As a result, at the same time Muslims were turning away from philosophy, Christians were beginning to embrace it. The writings of the ancient Greeks had been largely unknown in western Europe for some 600 years. Between the sixth and the twelfth centuries, European scholars had access to translations of only a few bits and pieces of Aristotle's and Plato's work. By the middle of the twelfth century, translations of some texts, most dealing with medicine and science, started introducing Europe to the intellectual legacy of the ancient world.

After Averroes' death, new translations of his works gave European scholars their first sustained taste of Aristotle's ideas and Averroes' interpretations of them. Jewish scholars translated some of them into Hebrew. These scholars were drawn to Averroes because he was held in great esteem by the Jewish philosopher Musa ibn Maymun (known in the West as Moses Maimonides [1135–1204]), who himself was a well-regarded interpreter of Aristotle. A contemporary of Averroes, Maimonides was born in Córdoba but fled al-Andalus after the Almohad rulers began forcing all non-Muslims to convert to Islam. Maimonides eventually settled in Egypt, where Jews enjoyed the usual religious freedom.

In the early thirteenth century, Averroes' work was also translated into Latin, the ancient Roman language well known to the learned. It was

Although Averroes' works were prohibited in Paris in the beginning of the 1200s, a philosophical movement in support of his writings was formed in the mid-1200s. One ardent supporter of Averroes and his commentaries on Aristotle was Siger of Brabant, who was a professor at the University of Paris. This seal for the University of Paris was made in the thirteenth century.

these translations that led the way to the popularization of Aristotle in western Europe. They were responsible for the full development of Scholasticism, a school of Christian thought that marked the golden age of philosophy in medieval Europe. Scholasticism sought a richer understanding of Christianity by examining its doctrines through reasoning and intellectual analysis.

During the thirteenth century, translations of Averroes' works became widely available at the universities that were springing up throughout Europe. Scholars were most interested in his commentaries on Aristotle. (His original works on philosophy and theology, such as *Incoherence of the Incoherence,* were far less widely read, probably because European Christians were not drawn to his musings on Islam.) In Europe, Averroes became so closely associated with Aristotle that he was often known merely as the Commentator.

Averroes' commentaries caused a stir among European intellectuals, in large part because of the challenge Greek philosophy seemed to pose to traditional religion. For more than 400 years, Muslim scholars had argued about whether philosophy and religion were compatible. Now, it was time for Christian thinkers to enter the debate.

The widespread interest in Averroes sparked a philosophical movement known as Averroism. Perhaps the most influential Averroist was Siger of Brabant (about 1240–1284). A professor at the University of Paris, he

OPTAVI ET DAT EI SEN SUS ET IVOCADI TOCIT IMESPS SAIE ET PPOSVI ILLA RE GNIS ET SEDIBVS

S IOHES EUAGELISTA

S MATHEUS EUAGEL

taught an interpretation of Aristotle that combined beliefs of Averroes and his fellow Muslim philosopher Avicenna.

CHALLENGING THE COMMENTATOR

Not surprisingly, Christian leaders saw Averroes as a threat. Often using arguments reminiscent of al-Ghazali's, they railed against his commentaries and the teaching of philosophy, claiming it was by its very nature incompatible with religious belief. One work challenging Averroes, written by the theologian Albert the Great in 1256, was specifically commissioned by the head of the Catholic Church, Pope Alexander IV.

In the thirteenth century, the Catholic Church made several efforts to ban Averroes' work. In 1210, the study of his commentaries on Aristotle was prohibited in Paris. But as the city grew into the world's greatest intellectual center, more and more people ignored the ban. In 1277, Étienne Tempier, bishop of Paris, with the encouragement of Pope

Andrea di Bonaiuto painted the fresco *Triumph of St. Thomas and Allegory of the Sciences* (1365–1368) in the Spanish Chapel of Santa Maria Novella in Florence, Italy. Pictured here is a detail from the fresco showing Thomas Aquinas. At his feet are Sabellius, Averroes, and Arius, who were considered heretics by the Catholic Church in the fourteenth century. While Aquinas was a student in Paris, he had studied Latin translations of Aristotle's and Averroes' works. Aquinas was greatly influenced by Averroes' composition style but disagreed with many of his opinions.

John XXI, launched another attack on Averroes' writings. He recorded a list of 219 ideas about God, the universe, and man's place in the universe. The church objected to the ideas, many of which were specifically aimed at the Averroists. Among the condemned ideas were the eternity of the world, the impossibility of miracles, and the superiority of philosophical truth over religious truth.

The Catholic Church also charged Siger of Brabant with heresy. Like other Averroists, he was accused of subscribing to the double-truth theory. This theory held that philosophy and religion provided such different ways of viewing the world that the same set of beliefs could be found true under one system and false under the other.

Averroes also came under attack by Thomas Aquinas (about 1224–1274), the leading Christian philosopher and theologian of the Middle Ages (the European name for the period of European history from AD 500 to about 1500). While a student of Albert the Great's at the University of Paris, Aquinas studied Aristotle and read the new Latin translations of Averroes' work. In 1270, he wrote *De Unitate Intellectus Contra Averroistas* (On the Unity of the Intellect Against the Averroists) in which he criticized the philosophy of Averroes and his follower Siger of Brabant. Aquinas's greatest work, however, was *Summa Theologica*, in which he tried to reconcile Aristotle's work with Christian beliefs.

DANTES ALIGHERIVS
Ex Pinacotheca Comitis Danielis Lisca
Patricii Veronensis, pictus quondam a
Bernardino India celebri pictore.

Mich. Angelus Cornale del.   M. Heulbrouck Sculp.

Poet Dante Alighieri (1265–1321) respected the philosophy and writings of Averroes and mentioned meeting the souls of Averroes and Avicenna in the first circle of hell in Canto IV of "The Inferno" from *The Divine Comedy*. Catholics burned Dante's book *De Monarchia* after his death because Pope John XXII believed that Dante was an Averroist.

THE END OF AVERROISM

Aquinas's criticisms and the Catholic Church's condemnations slowed the spread of Averroism in Paris. Averroes' popularity was also diminished because Aquinas commissioned

Averroes in the Arts

Reflecting his importance in Western culture, Averroes is referred to in two of the greatest literary works of the fourteenth century. In the prologue of *The Canterbury Tales*, the English poet Geoffrey Chaucer offers a list of medical authorities that includes Averroes. The reference makes clear that even 200 years after Averroes' death, his medical writings were still well known throughout Europe.

Averroes also makes an appearance in *The Divine Comedy* by Italian poet Dante Alighieri. In this poem, Dante takes a journey through hell, purgatory, and heaven. In hell, he encounters Saladin, the Kurdish warrior who ruled Egypt and led a Muslim army that captured Jerusalem from the hands of Christian crusaders in 1187. Around Saladin, Dante saw "his philosophic family" of great Greek and Muslim thinkers.

There, nearest him, and before the rest,
I saw Socrates and Plato . . .

I saw Dioscorides, the good taxonomist
Of plants, and I saw Orpheus,
Tully and Linus, and Seneca the moralist;

Euclid the geometer, and Ptolemy,
Hippocrates, Galen, Avicenna,
And Averroes who made the Great Commentary.

(continued on next page)

Raphael, another great Italian artist, also paid tribute to Averroes. In his fresco *School of Athens* (1510–1511), in the Stanza della Signatura in the Vatican Palace in Italy, Raphael depicted Plato and Aristotle in the center, surrounded by dozens of philosophers influenced by their teachings. At the far left, Averroes appears, dressed in a green robe and white turban, intently looking over the shoulder of the Greek philosopher Pythagoras as he writes in a book. No image of Averroes made in his lifetime has survived, so Raphael's portrait is based solely on the painter's imagination.

In 1997, Averroes became an unlikely screen hero in *Destiny*, a film by famed Egyptian director Youssef Chahine. The romantic adventure is set in al-Andalus during the period when Averroes fell out of the caliph's favor. Chahine celebrates Averroes as a man of wisdom and conviction, even though his beliefs place him in harm's way.

This detail from Raphael's *School of Athens* shows Averroes (wearing a turban).

William of Moerbeke to translate Aristotle's work directly into Latin. Many scholars came to favor these translations, and as a result, Averroes' paraphrases and interpretations of Aristotle's works lost some of their influence in Europe.

Nevertheless, Averroes continued to attract scholarly attention in Italy, particularly in the city of Padua. The most influential Averroist in Padua was John of Jandun (about 1286–1328). John of Jandun called Averroes "the most perfect and glorious physician, friend and fearless defender of the truth." Another Italian student of Averroes was the great poet Dante Alighieri (1265–1321). Averroes' philosophy greatly influenced his political treatise *De Monarchia* (On World Government). After Dante's death, Dante was accused of Averroism, and Pope John XXII ordered the public burning of copies of *De Monarchia*.

Averroism continued well into the Renaissance. Lasting from the thirteenth to the sixteenth centuries, this period saw a sustained interest in the work of Greek and Roman writers. As the great commentator of Aristotle, Averroes remained an important figure for Renaissance scholars. But at the same time, the Renaissance also led to decreased interest in his work. More and more scholars learned Greek in order to have a more direct understanding of ancient texts. Because Averroes only knew Aristotle from Arabic translations, some students of philosophy came to question the authenticity of his interpretations.

In 1852, the French philosopher and historian Joseph Ernest Renan wrote *Averroes and the Averroists*, in which he analyzed Averroes' influence on Western philosophy. Renan's book, which he originally wrote for his doctoral degree, helped to rekindle interest in Averroes' commentaries on the Greek philosophers.

REVIVING AVERROES

Interest in Averroes was revived during the nineteenth century, in large part because of the work of French philosopher Joseph Ernest Renan (1823–1892). In 1852,

Renan published *Averroes and the Averroists*, which chronicled Averroes' influence on the Western world. Some of Renan's claims, however, have been questioned by later scholars. He drew especially sharp criticism for his theory that the Averroists of the thirteenth century saw the philosophy of Averroes and Aristotle as being in complete opposition to Christian doctrine. Many scholars have also raised doubts about Renan's idea that these Averroists amounted to a kind of secret sect who hoped to launch a stealth attack on Christianity. Nevertheless, Renan excited a renewed interest in Averroes among European scholars that continues until this day.

Renan's work also inspired a study of Averroes by Muslim scholar Farah Antun. In 1903, Antun wrote *Ibn Rushd and His Philosophy*, in which he attempted to link Averroes' rationalism with modern secularism. Antun was one of the leaders of Nahda, a movement that sought to combine Muslim and non-Muslim culture. Members of this movement embraced Averroes because, in their interpretation, his work exposed the differences between philosophy and religion. This served their goal of working to separate the church and the state in Muslim lands. Antun's book was highly controversial but ultimately had little impact on Averroes' reputation in the East. With the exception of most Muslim philosophical circles, Averroes remains an obscure Muslim figure. Even today, the history of Islamic thought largely ignores Averroes' contributions.

In Western society, though, Averroes has left an indelible mark. He is still studied as one of the most comprehensive and intriguing interpreters of the work of Aristotle. But even more significantly, Averroes is seen as a crucial bridge between ancient and modern philosophy because of his role in introducing Europe to Greek thought.

TIMELINE

1126

Averroes (Ibn Rushd) is born in Córdoba in al-Andalus (Muslim Spain).

1146

The Almohad dynasty invades and rules al-Andalus.

1153

Averroes travels to Marrakesh and begins to study astronomy.

1169

Averroes completes the medical treatise *Generalities in Medicine*. Averroes' friend Ibn Tufayl introduces him to the Almohad caliph, Abu Yaqub Yusuf, who commissions him to write commentaries on Aristotle. Averroes becomes a qadi (a religious judge) in Seville.

1169–1190

Averroes writes his major works on Aristotle.

1180

Averroes is appointed grand qadi of Córdoba.

1182

Averroes becomes the physician to the caliph.

1184

Averroes completes *Incoherence of the Incoherence.*

1191

Averroes completes his commentary on Plato's *Republic.*

1195

The Almohad authorities banish Averroes and burn his works.

1197

The caliph allows Averroes to return to Marrakesh and lifts the ban on his writing.

1198

Averroes dies in Marrakesh, Morocco. His body is later returned to Córdoba for burial.

GLOSSARY

al-Andalus A portion of present-day Spain that was under Muslim rule from the eighth to the fifteenth centuries.

Averroism The thirteenth-century philosophical movement in Europe that was based on Averroes' commentaries on Aristotle.

caliph Successor to the prophet Muhammad. A ruler of the Muslim Empire.

commentary An extended written interpretation or explanation.

dynasty A succession of rulers from the same family.

emanationist Relating to a theory about the creation of the world, in which God was the starting point for a series of causes and effects that make up the structure of reality.

empire A group of territories or nations, often united by conquest and ruled by a single leader.

heresy An opinion that contradicts accepted religious beliefs.

Hijra The prophet Muhammad's flight from Mecca (Makkah) to Medina (Madinah) in 622, which marks the beginning of the Muslim calendar.

Islam A monotheistic religion based on the words of the Qur'an and the teachings of the prophet Muhammad.

mosque A Muslim house of worship.

Muslim A believer in Islam.

mystical Relating to a spiritual realm not discernible by the senses or by reason.

philosophy The study of the nature of reality and principles underlying thinking and being.

qadi A Muslim judge who administers rulings based on the sharia.

Qur'an (Koran) The sacred book of Islam, believed to be the word of God revealed to the prophet Muhammad.

sharia The body of sacred Islamic law.

theology The study of God and religion.

FOR MORE INFORMATION

Arab World and Islamic Resources
P.O. Box 174
Abiquiu, NM 87510
(510) 704-0517
Web site: http://www.awaironline.org

Council on Islamic Education
9300 Gardenia Street, B-3
Fountain Valley, CA 92708
(714) 839-2929
Web site: http://www.cie.org

International Museum of Muslim Cultures
117 East Pascagoula Street
Jackson, MS 39201
(601) 960-0440
Web site: http://www.muslimmuseum.org

The Islamic Information Centre
460 Stapleton Road, Eastville
Bristol BS5 6PA
United Kingdom
(011) 7902 0037
Web site: http://www.islamicinformationcentre.co.uk

Metropolitan Museum of Art
Islamic Art Division
1000 Fifth Avenue
New York, NY 10028
(212) 535-7710
Web site: http://www.metmuseum.org/Works_Of_Art/
    department.asp?dep=14

WEB SITES

Due to the changing nature of Internet links, the Rosen
Publishing Group, Inc., has developed an online list of Web
sites related to the subject of this book. This site is updated
regularly. Please use this link to access the list:

http://www.rosenlinks.com/gmps/aver

FOR FURTHER READING

Armstrong, Karen. *Islam: A Short History*. Rev. ed. New York, NY: Modern Library, 2002.

Doak, Robin. *Empire of the Islamic World*. New York, NY: Facts on File, 2004.

Hayes, John R., ed. *The Genius of Arab Civilization*. 3rd ed. New York, NY: New York University Press, 1992.

Inati, Shams C. "Baghdad in the Golden Age: A Historical Tour." *Iraq: Its History, People, and Politics*, ed. Shams C. Inati. Amherst, NY: Prometheus Books, 2003.

Marston, Elsa. *Muhammad of Mecca: Prophet of Islam*. New York, NY: Franklin Watts, 2001.

Menocal, María Rosa. *The Ornament of the World: How Muslims, Jews, and Christians Created a Culture of Tolerance in Medieval Spain*. Boston, MA: Little, Brown and Company, 2002.

BIBLIOGRAPHY

Arnaldez, Roger. *Averroes: A Rationalist in Islam*. Translated
by David Streight. Notre Dame, IN: University of Notre
Dame Press, 2000.

Averroes. *Faith and Reason in Islam*. Translated by
Ibrahim Najjar. Oxford, England: Oneworld
Publications, 2001.

Esposito, John L., ed. *The Oxford History of Islam*. New
York, NY: Oxford University Press, 1999.

Fakhry, Majid. *A Short Introduction to Islamic Philosophy,
Theology, and Mysticism*. Oxford, England: Oneworld
Publications, 1997.

Fakhry, Majid. *Averroes: His Life, Works and Influence*.
Oxford, England: Oneworld Publications, 2001.

Hayes, John R., ed. *The Genius of Arab Civilization*.
3rd ed. New York, NY: New York University
Press, 1992.

Hourani, George F. *Averroes: On the Harmony of
Religion and Philosophy*. London, England: Lowe &
Byrondone, 1976.

Leaman, Oliver. *Averroes and His Philosophy*. Richmond,
England: Curzon, 1998.

Leaman, Oliver. *A Brief Introduction to Islamic Philosophy*.
Cambridge, England: Polity Press, 1999.

Menocal, María Rosa. *The Ornament of the World: How Muslims, Jews, and Christians Created a Culture of Tolerance in Medieval Spain.* Boston, MA: Little, Brown and Company, 2002.

Stone, Caroline. "Doctor, Philosopher, Renaissance Man." *Saudi Aramco World*, Vol. 54, No. 3, May/June 2003, pp. 8–15.

INDEX

About the Author

Liz Sonneborn is a writer, living in Brooklyn, New York. A graduate of Swarthmore College, she has written more than fifty books for children and adults. Specializing in American and world history, she has a particular interest in the cultures and philosophy of the ancient world. Her books include *The Ancient Kushites*, and *The Ancient Aztecs*.

About the Consultant

Munir A. Shaikh, executive director of the Council on Islamic Education (CIE), reviewed this book. The CIE is a non-advocacy, academic research institute that provides consulting services and academic resources related to teaching about world history and world religions. http://www.cie.org.

Photo Credits

Cover, p. 90 Scala/Art Resource, NY; p. 7 © Hans Georg Roth/Corbis; p. 9 The Granger Collection, New York; pp. 12, 50, 52, 54, 55, 86 Bibliothèque nationale de France; pp. 15, 64, 95 Erich Lessing/Art Resource, NY; pp. 16–17 The Pierpont Morgan Library/Art Resource, NY; p. 19 © Kazuyoshi Nomachi/HAGA/The Image Works; p. 20 © The British Museum/HIP/The Image Works; p. 23 Werner Forman Archive/Oriental Collection, State University Library, Leiden, the Netherlands, Location: 17 © 2004 Werner Forman/TopFoto/The Image Works; pp. 26, 39, 57, 74, 94, 95 © Background tiles courtesy of Mosaic House, New York; p. 28 © The British Library: Royal 16 G. VI f.185v; p. 33 Mezquita (Great Mosque) Córdoba, Spain, Index/Bridgeman Art Library; p. 36 Bibliothèque Nationale, Paris, France, Archives Charmet/Bridgeman Art Library; p. 38 Courtesy of MuslimHeritage.com; pp. 40, 88 Giraudon/Art Resource, NY; p. 42 The Art Archive/National Museum Damascus Syria/Dagli Orti; p.45 ArkReligion.com/TRIP; p. 49 Alinari/Art Resource, NY; p. 60 by permission of the Syndics of Cambridge University Library, Class-mark Or.165 (8), f. 1v; p. 67 © The British Library: Add. 27261 f.362v; p. 70 Asian and Middle Eastern Division, The New York Public Library, Astor, Lenox and Tilden Foundations; p. 73 Courtesy National Library of Medicine; p. 76 Bildarchiv Preussischer Kulturbesitz/Art Resource, NY; pp. 78, 93 Library of Congress Prints and Photographs Division; p. 81 © Mary Evans Picture Library/The Image Works; pp. 84–85 Toledo Cathedral, Castile, Spain/Bridgeman Art Library; p. 97 © Hulton-Deutsch Collection/Corbis.

Designer: Les Kanturek; Editor: Kathy Kuhtz Campbell
Photo Researcher: Gabriel Caplan